IMAGES OF SCOTLAND

EDINBURGH
NEW TOWN

IMAGES OF SCOTLAND

EDINBURGH NEW TOWN

TEMPUS

Frontispiece: Waterloo Place, *c.* 1900.

First published 2007

Tempus Publishing
Cirencester Road, Chalford,
Stroud, Gloucestershire, GL6 8PE
www.tempus-publishing.com

Tempus Publishing is an imprint of NPI Media Group

British Library Cataloguing in Publication Data.
A catalogue record for this book is available from the British Library.

ISBN 978 0 7524 4363 8

Typesetting and origination by NPI Media Group
Printed in Great Britain

Contents

Acknowledgements

Thanks to my husband James for boundless moral and technical support; Fiona Myles and my colleagues in the Edinburgh Room for their help; to Peter Stubbs, photographer and web author of www.edinphoto.org.uk for being a wonderful source of information; to Wendy French, babysitter and proof reader extraordinaire; to Lindsay Levy (the new Duchess of Queen Street) for endless enthusiasm.

My gratitude to the following photographers and families who kindly gave me their permission to use photographs in this book – the *Evening News* and *Scotsman* newspapers; Mrs Barbara Hill; Mrs Frances Porteous; Kevin Wheelan.

Thanks also to the Edinburgh Photographic Society (EPS), who allowed me to use some of their photographs in this compilation. The EPS was formed in 1861 and has been supporting both professional and amateur photographers ever since. From their beautiful premises at Great King Street in Edinburgh's New Town, they provide darkroom, studio and library facilities and have weekly lectures on photography. They have the most wonderful collection of photography and regularly display work both on their website, www.edinburgh-photographicsociety.co.uk, and at regular exhibitions. Immense thanks to Anne Rogers and the EPS committee for all their help.

Every effort has been made to locate copyright holders and seek permission for the use of all photographs in this book. If we have missed anyone then we apologise here.

Introduction

The New Town arose, growing from day to day until Edinburgh became one of the most handsome and picturesque cities in Europe.

James Nasmyth

Edinburgh is an ancient settlement originating from an Iron Age fort on top of a volcanic ridge. Over time, the population grew, space became limited and settlement was restricted to the ridge, as expansion was curtailed by the deep ravines and swamps that surrounded the site. A unique society developed within this limited space, with all strata of society often living within the same buildings; aristocracy at the top and the lower classes at the bottom. By the eighteenth century, conditions were becoming unbearable, due to overcrowding, disease and the hazardous condition of some of the old buildings.

In 1752, a pamphlet was issued containing the ideas of George Drummond, the Lord Provost, for extending the royalty of the city to the lands of the north and south, enlarging the city and turning the Nor Loch into a canal. The ideas expounded in the leaflet were not universally popular and it took another twenty years before any progress was made towards them. Drummond knew that expansion was not possible without a way to bridge the Nor Loch and the depression that it was sited in. He also knew that those who were not keen to build outside the city's walls would still find the idea of a bridge, linking with the Wester Road to Leith, a pleasing prospect. Drummond therefore pushed forward the building of the North Bridge under the guise of improving access to the Port of Leith. Building began in 1764 and with it the idea of access to the lands of the north became a reality.

Just two years later, a competition was advertised to design a residential suburb of the city on the land of Barefoot's Park, which bounded the Nor Loch. This began a chain of building that lasted from 1767 till the 1890s and created the largest area of neo-classical eighteenth and nineteenth-century architecture in the world. Edinburgh's New Town, as it became known, is also one of the most architecturally intact sites of its type. Its uniqueness resulted in it being made a UNESCO World Heritage Site in 1995.

Although the building of the New Town can be viewed primarily as a need to escape the conditions of the Old, it was brought about by deeper reasons than this. Edinburgh was facing one of its darkest times; the removal of the royal court to London by James VI in 1603, coupled with the loss of the Scottish Parliament in 1707, had left a demoralised city lacking in prestige. Its place as a significant capital city was threatened, so it simply reinvented itself. Edinburgh and its elite wanted the world to sit up and admire their city. This positive response in the face of adversity is understandable too when you consider the cultural phenomenon of the Scottish Enlightenment that was centred on Edinburgh. The city became

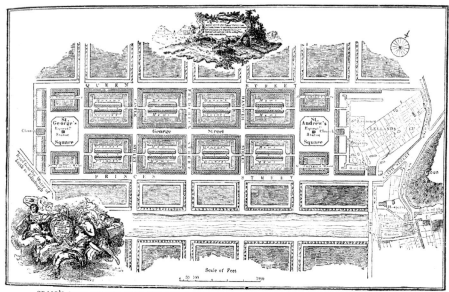

CRAIG'S PLAN OF THE NEW STREETS AND SQUARES INTENDED FOR THE CITY OF EDINBURGH.

Craig's map of the New Town, 1767. Here we see James Craig's final design for his New Town. It was to be a self-contained suburb, bounded by gardens to the north and south and originally, there was to be a canal flowing through the Nor Loch basin. The names for the streets and squares have been finalised; on earlier versions Queen Street and Princes Street were known as Forth Street and St Giles Street.

a 'hotbed of genius', where moral philosophy, history and economics were debated by the most learned men of their generation. Edinburgh became not a place for problems, but for well thought-out solutions.

The creation of the New Town saw the mass exodus of the gentry from the Old Town. They were soon followed by the middling classes, leaving the crumbling homes of the original city to its poorest inhabitants. The New Town was conceived of merely as a residential suburb, with the commercial aspects of the city to be carried on from the High Street as always. Returning to the decaying Old Town however proved unappealing to those who had flitted to the New and gradually, commercial and government activities were leached from their original settings to more desirable sites. The creation of new suburbs was an unstoppable process, with scheme after scheme being implemented. Given the confines of this book, it has been impossible to cover every New Town phase. Most notably, those that have not been included are the developments to the south: the Dean Estate, Deanhaugh and the Raeburn Estate. Also, it has sometimes proved difficult to define which streets come under which particular scheme, as many of the sources contradict themselves.

All the images in this book come from the collections of the Edinburgh Room, Central Library on George IV Bridge. The Edinburgh Room has the most comprehensive collection in the world of material relating to Edinburgh. A core part of their collection is illustrative and presents a pictorial history of the city in prints, photographs, paintings, maps, drawings and slides. The contents of this book represent a tiny proportion of the 150,000 illustrations held by the Edinburgh Room, which cover all facets of the city's geography, history and culture. If you have any enquiries relating to the images in this book, please contact edinburgh.room@edinburgh.gov.uk, or telephone 0131 242 8030.

one

Bridges

Bridges were essential to the creation of the New Town and their construction heralded the end of the Old Town's grip on the boundaries of Edinburgh. Kept compact and clinging to the volcanic crag and tail, Edinburgh had been unable to expand to the north or south due to the geography of deep valleys, marshy land and the Nor Loch. The building of the North Bridge in 1765 provided a link across the valley to the lands of the north and gave the access needed to begin constructing the New Town, outside the barriers of the Old. Prior to building the bridge, it was necessary to drain part of the Nor Loch to allow a firm foundation to be built to support the three stone arches of the new bridge. Its construction did not go smoothly however, as a design flaw led to a partial collapse which killed five workers and delayed its opening. The 1,134ft bridge finally opened in 1772, after delays and protracted arguments between the architect, William Mylne, and the council over the price.

The long-awaited bridge was only to last a little over 100 years; after this time it became necessary to replace it with another construction. The redevelopment of Waverley station called for the building of a new bridge to allow for major remodelling of the station. The original stone one was therefore replaced by a steel-girder construction designed by Sir William Arrol. It cost more than £81,000 to construct and was built from 1894-7.

Not as grand in its construction or planning, the Earthen Mound was also important in allowing access to the lands of the growing New Town. The construction of the Mound was begun by individuals who no doubt owned property to the west of Princes Street and found it inconvenient to go via the North Bridge. The practice was started of dumping the rubble excavated to create the foundations for the houses on Princes Street into the Nor Loch valley, thus creating a rough causeway. In 1781 the town council formalised this practice and by 1830, a substantial raised road had been created. This space was also to provide land for the building of the Royal Institution (now the Royal Scottish Academy) and the National Gallery of Scotland (opened in 1836 and 1859 respectively).

The North Bridge from Regent Road by Thomas Begbie, 1857. This photo shows the original North Bridge which opened in 1772, comprising of three stone arches spanning 1,134ft. Under the arches lay the fish and flesh markets.

South side of the North Bridge, 1895. Showing the underside of the original bridge, this is where the train tracks come under the bridge heading for Waverley train station. The top of a train wagon can just be seen as well as a billboard with publicity for Professor T.A. Kennedy, a spoof mesmerist and self-styled 'King Laugh Maker of the World'.

The North Bridge at the High Street, looking north by Alexander A. Inglis, 1896. Most of these buildings on the south side of the bridge were replaced in the early 1900s, largely by the imposing Carlton Hotel that was originally built as the Bon Marché department store and later taken over by Patrick Thomson's store.

Above: Laying the foundation stone of the new North Bridge, 1896.

Left: Removal of the old North Bridge and laying the foundation stone of the new, 1896. The original stone-built bridge was replaced by a steel-girder construction started in 1895. Here we can see the foundation stone being laid by the Lord Provost Andrew McDonald. The main reason for the construction of the new bridge was to allow Waverley station to be rebuilt and enlarged. The North British Railway Company did in fact pay for a third of the costs since its remodelling was essential to their plans.

High Street corner on the North Bridge by Alexander A. Inglis, *c.* 1896. The buildings at the end were demolished three years after this picture was taken to construct the *Scotsman* newspaper offices. The newspaper moved in the 1990s to a new building in the Canongate and the old one has now been turned into the Scotsman Hotel.

William Morton & Sons, 30 North Bridge, 1894. This was a very successful business of ribbon, lace, glove, artificial flower and millinery warehouses at North Bridge and Lothian Road. The North Bridge shop operated for a long time from 1882-1935, but was outlived by the Lothian Road branch.

William Tait & Co., 5 North Bridge, *c.* 1896. This row of shops includes William Tait & Co., a button, trimming, Berlin wool and hosiery warehouse which operated from the North Bridge from 1890-1914.

A huge line of people, apparently queuing for the J. Stewart Lamb sale on North Bridge at the High Street, *c.* 1910. They were obviously not able to resist the draw of the 'save on your blouses' poster. J. Stewart Lamb was a millinery, mantle and dress warehouse operating from 56 North Bridge from 1907-54.

An image of the North Bridge, showing the North British Hotel under construction, 1901. With its 195ft clock tower, this opulent Edwardian hotel was set to become a key landmark in Edinburgh. It opened in 1902 and was renamed the Balmoral ninety years later.

Scotsman Steps by George Malcolm, c. 1930. Climbing up the Scotsman Steps that lead from Market Street to the North Bridge, beside the Scotsman building.

'The Earthen Mound' by John Le Conte, 1835. This watercolour illustrates how rough the construction of the Mound was initially; it literally is just a mound of earth, rather at odds with the elegant arches of the North Bridge that can be seen to the right of the painting. The Mound, however, was always a place of entertainment, whether of a high-brow nature, provided by the galleries at its base, or the more populist entertainments of menageries, circuses and dioramas. The two circular rotundas that can be seen at the head of the Mound contained the Marshall's and Adcock's Panoramas. They displayed huge 360-degree painted scenes of history, nature and the world. Wombwell's Animal Menagerie also inhabited the land to the north of the panoramas.

The Mound by the *Scotsman*, c. 1955. No longer a rough mound of earth, the beautifully landscaped road snakes its way down towards the New Town. Princes Street too has changed dramatically – gone is the line of uniform houses with their flat fronts and matching roof lines, now there is a mixture of the tall and short, the tasteful and disgraceful from a variety of different periods.

George Brown, the Mound Book Store on Bank Street, *c.* 1905. This shop opened in 1879 and existed for almost 100 years until 1971. Bank Street leads down from the High Street to the head of the Mound. It was built in 1798 and named after the Bank of Scotland who soon made their headquarters here.

Magistrates at the Mound awaiting Masonic procession, 1896. Still a site of many processions today, here large crowds gather to watch the Masonic procession in honour of the laying of the foundation stone of the new North Bridge. At the top of the Mound are the two towers of the General Assembly Hall of the Church of Scotland. The building is also shared with New College, Edinburgh University's Faculty of Divinity. The imposing building was designed by William Henry Playfair and begun in 1846. The Assembly Hall was used as a temporary home for the Scottish Parliament from 1999-2004.

Concert party at the Mound by Ada J. Anderson, *c.* 1918. This photograph most probably dates from the end of the First World War. A concert party of clowns can be seen entertaining the crowds in front of a rest hut offering refreshments to soldiers and sailors. The domes of the Bank of Scotland can be seen at the head of Mound. Built in 1806, Richard Crichton's Corinthian design looks impressive from its viewpoint overlooking the Nor Loch valley. Its construction, however, proved to be expensive as it was not constructed on solid ground, but on the loose earth of the Mound, and had to be extensively under-built.

Royal Scottish Academy, the Mound, *c.* 1925. The Royal Institution was built in 1822 and designed by William Playfair. As with Crichton's Bank of Scotland, Playfair had to cope with the unstable nature of the Mound and cleverly constructed his building on piles. Little more than ten years after its construction though, Playfair was asked to redesign the building to create more space. Initially the building served as home to many societies, including the Board of Manufacturers, the Royal Society of Edinburgh and the Society of Antiquities of Scotland. It is now the Royal Scottish Academy.

two

Nor
Loch Basin

Although a subject of debate, it is likely that the Nor Loch was man-made and that King James III turned the already marshy land into a defensive lake for the castle by building a dam at the eastern end and utilising the spring from St Margaret's well. It stretched from just past where the North Bridge is today to St Cuthbert's church in the west. The Nor Loch was a hindrance to expanding the city. Bridges were one way of overcoming the problem, but there were other issues about the loch rather than just crossing it. At first it was a picturesque addition to the landscape, but by the Middle Ages, it had become a dumping ground for the rubbish and sewage of the city, turning it into a 'noxious lake'. The stench was overpowering, with methane gas rising from the putrid waters. The loch became an unsavoury area, bounded by the local slaughter houses. In addition, it had a reputation for being a dumping ground for victims of murder and a suicide spot. It was also where many of Edinburgh's suspected witches met their end, in so-called dunking 'trials'.

This was not something that the upper classes of Edinburgh wished to have beside their new city. Calls for something to be done with the Nor Loch began early in the eighteenth century. In 1723, an Act of Parliament was passed allowing for the loch to be turned into a canal and again in 1752, this idea was included in ideas put forth for the extension of the city. However, it was not until 1763 that Provost George Drummond pushed forward the draining of some of the eastern end of the loch to allow for the building of the North Bridge. Progress was slow; the section west of the Mound was still a swamp until 1817.

Initially then, the land created by the removal of the loch served as private gardens. However, later in 1876, it became a public park. The site covers almost twenty-eight acres and is divided in two by the Mound; creating East and West Princes Street Gardens. The gardens are home to the Floral Clock, Ross Bandstand and many monuments to Edinburgh's great and good. Perhaps the most famous monument in Scotland resides in East Princes Street Gardens – the Scott Monument. The enormous Gothic creation dwarfs the surrounding landscape, standing 180ft tall. Designed by George Kemp as a memorial to Sir Walter Scott, the foundation stone was laid in 1840, eight years after Scott's death.

The development of Waverley station began just after the end of the Georgian period and so cannot be considered to have been concurrent with the creation of the New Town. Its existence though was completely dependant on the works carried out to create the New Town. The station and the railway lines running to the west sit neatly in the basin created by the removal of the Nor Loch. The draining of the loch and availability of the resulting lands coincided with the birth of rail travel in Britain. From 1840 onwards, three railway companies vied for business from the area and they assumed the collective name of 'Waverley' from the 1850s after Sir Walter Scott's *Waverley* novels and the proximity of the Scott Monument. The companies amalgamated in 1868 under the name of the North British Railway and the site was redeveloped, creating the Victorian station we can see today. It swept away many of the produce markets that existed on the site and required the rebuilding of the North Bridge to accommodate its later expansion. It now occupies a 25 acre site and is one of the largest stations in Britain.

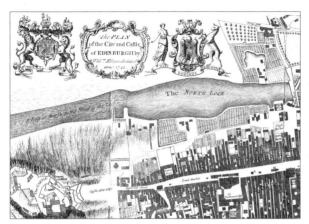

Edgar's map of Edinburgh, 1742. Completed prior to the building of the New Town, this map illustrates the expanse of the Nor Loch and how it effectively prevented the Old Town from expanding any further to the north. Along the eastern edges of the loch there are gardens. Further to the west however, the ground was too boggy to be used for anything. The area around the loch would have been most unpleasant as the rubbish from the Old Town was dumped into its waters, creating a putrid smell.

A view from the Earthen Mound, 1816. This image beautifully illustrates the large bowl-shaped valley that was left after the draining of the Nor Loch. It is also interesting to see the uniformity of the buildings along Princes Street to the right. Here it is as originally designed – a residential street full of houses. At the end of the valley lies St Cuthbert's church and the dome of St George's parish church can be seen behind the houses of Princes Street.

View of the new bridge of Edinburgh with the adjacent building of the Old and New Towns from the west by Thomas Donaldson, 1775. An early view over the drained Nor Loch showing the Old Town on the left connected by the arches of the North Bridge, to the emergent New Town on the right. Thomas Donaldson was a limner (portrait painter) and engraver who was allowed to enter the sanctuary of Holyrood to escape his debts.

Above: Opening ceremony of the Scott Monument, 1846. It took four years to build the Scott Monument from the laying of the foundation stone in 1840 to 1844, when the final stone was placed on the top by the designer's son, Thomas Kemp. This image however, must date from the official inauguration on 15 August 1846. It is testimony to Scott's popularity that, not only was the monument constructed, but that its opening was marked by the great sea of people seen here, stretching the length of East Princes Street Gardens.

Opposite below: East Princes Street Gardens; view across the gardens to the National Gallery of Scotland and the Royal Institution (now the Royal Scottish Academy), *c.* 1890. The ornate steps lead down into the valley that once contained the Nor Loch.

Right: Scott Monument under construction by Francis M. Chrystal, 1844.

Below: Building of the Walter Scott Monument, in the early stages by Francis M Chrystal, *c.* 1844. These images show the Scott Monument under construction. Sir Walter Scott had died in 1832 and immediately there was public calling for a monument to be built to his memory. An architectural competition was organised and won by George Miekle Kemp, a joiner, who based his design on Melrose Abbey, a place which had been so loved by Scott. In the centre of the design is a statue of Scott carved in white marble by Sir John Steell. It is twice life-size and depicts Scott with his favourite staghound, Maida, sitting beside him.

Left: The Scott Monument and Princes Street, *c.* 1853. Like a great rocket rising out of Princes Street Gardens, the Scott Monument stands a little over 200ft high. It is possible to climb up a staircase that is located in the south-west section of pillars and climb the 287 steps up to the highest gallery. The intricate design of the monument also includes sixty-four niches where statues of characters from Scott's novels have been placed. It took until 1881 to fill every niche on the monument. There are also carvings of the heads of other famous Scottish poets such as Robert Burns and Allan Ramsay.

Below: Scott Monument and Princes Street Gardens, *c.* 1905. A very tropical-looking Princes Street Gardens complete with palm trees. The immaculately looked-after beds prove the gardener is hard at work and a watering machine can be seen on the grass.

East Princes Street Gardens by Thomas C.A. Inglis, 1953. This picture was taken on an apparently beautiful afternoon for a chat in the gardens, which were a common meeting spot for the populus of Edinburgh. The buildings in the background include the two towers of the General Assembly Hall on the right and the dome of the Bank of Scotland headquarters on the left.

Charabanc trip to the Scott Monument from Grimsby by Francis C. Inglis, *c.* 1925. Charabancs first appeared in the early 1900s and were a type of open-topped bus. It was a very popular pastime in the 1920s and '30s to go on charabanc trips and was often organised as a work outing.

West Princes Street Gardens; recording a very popular concert at the bandstand in Princes Street Gardens, 1905. The bandstand was installed in 1877 but was later replaced by the much larger Ross Bandstand in 1934. It is still used as a venue for concerts today, particularly during the summer festivals.

Right: Ross Fountain, Princes Street Gardens by Mary P.A. Wilkinson, 1954. The iron fountain was made in France for the 1862 Great Exhibition in London. As with many such events, the exhibits were sold at the end of the exhibition. The fountain was bought by a local gun maker called Daniel Ross. He had a great interest in science and art and perhaps was drawn to the piece as three of the featured nymphs represent science, poetry and the arts. It was shipped to Leith in bits and finally installed in Princes Street Gardens in 1872.

Below: The Floral Clock in Princes Street Gardens by Mary P.A. Wilkinson, 1954. Edinburgh's Floral Clock is the oldest in the world, having been created in 1904. With a circumference of 36ft, it is huge, taking about 40,000 plants to cover it. Most of the plants are from the *semperviven* family (chosen for their small size) and these even cover the clock's hands. The clock has a working electric movement and a cuckoo that calls on the hour.

Waverley station and Waverley Bridge, as originally constructed by J.G. Tunny, 1854. Here is the Waverley Bridge as it was originally constructed prior to rebuilding in 1868 and 1895. This image was also taken before the construction of Cockburn Street in 1859 so the Bridge ends at a T-junction rather than carrying on up the wonderful curve of Cockburn Street to the High Street. Calder's Traveller's Hotel and Railway Station Hotel in Market Street can also be seen, as well as the Bank of Scotland prior to its alterations in 1868. The sheds to the front of the bridge are occupied by George Gordon and Pickford & Co. carting contractors and were well placed for picking up business from the station.

Waverley Bridge, works in progress, 1896. The Waverley Bridge was originally just an embankment made of earth. Like the Mound, it developed to give access to the New Town and was originally known as 'Little Mound'. In 1844, a proper stone bridge was constructed and it was named 'Waverley' – no doubt because of its vicinity to the nearly-finished Scott Monument and so was named after Scott's *Waverley* novels.

Waverley Bridge by Francis M. Chrystal, *c.* 1930.

Waverley Bridge showing the entrance to Waverley station, *c.* 1906. These images of the Waverley Bridge are looking towards the premises of Renton's drapers and furnishers and R.W. Forsyth's department store. Renton's was previously the Edinburgh Hotel and was later demolished, becoming the site of the C & A building. Forsyth's finally closed in the 1980s, but the building was taken over by the Burton Group.

Right: The south front of the Waverley Market by George Morham, *c.* 1880. A group of young boys stand in the street outside the Waverley Market. This wonderful cast-iron structure was finally completely removed in 1974, as it was deemed to be unsafe. The building at the far right of the picture has boxes of vegetables for sale outside it.

Below: Waverley station platform with Calton Gaol in the background by Dr Francis Smart, 1889. This atmospheric photograph of a platform at Waverley station shows the scene when a train has just arrived and the passengers are getting off. The smoke from the steam train competes with the smoke from the chimneys of the houses at Lower Calton. Towering above the platform is the Governor's House and Calton Gaol.

Opposite above: The roof of the Waverley Market by George Morham, *c.* 1880.

Opposite below: Inside the Waverley Market by George Morham, *c.* 1880. These two images show an amazingly constructed multi-purpose building with the utilitarian market underneath and the beautifully landscaped gardens above. The interior shot shows how the glass 'wells' let light into the building from the roof and that glass was also used for much of the visible walls, compensating for the building being sunk into the ground and having no light on two of its sides.

Left: Waverley station by P.B. Browning, 1955.

Below: Waverley station by Peter Frew, 1956. These two images of the interior of Waverley station date from the 1950s. Three railway companies operated from this site in the 1840s. In 1854 however, Waverley station was created and the site went on to be extended and rebuilt several times between 1869-1900, leading to the Victorian building that we see today.

three

First New Town

The town council launched a competition in 1766 for the laying-out of the lands to the north. The six entries were judged by the Lord Provost and the architect John Adam. Surprisingly, the winning entry was from a very young architect, James Craig, who was a mere twenty-three years old. It appears that the plan required some adjustments, but a rectified design was put before the King in 1767.

The design was quite simple – in fact Craig has been criticised for his lack of imagination and creativity. It was rectangular in shape, consisting of three large parallel streets with three smaller cross streets, terminating in a square at each end. Where it might not have been 'cutting-edge' design, Craig did make the most of the surrounding landscape. George Street was sited upon the ridge that ran across the site and Princes Street on the existing Lang Gait Road. The most important feature was the view and Craig exploited this by having Princes and Queen Streets single-sided; so to have open views of Edinburgh Castle and down to the Forth respectively. The original buildings were also a little monotonous in design, consisting of three-storey town houses with little variation. By the early nineteenth century however, most of the original buildings had been altered or replaced by commercial properties, all set in Craig's original layout.

The naming of the streets in the plan was a tribute to the monarchy and the infant Treaty of Union, which joined the English and Scottish parliaments. It was not long after the Jacobite Rebellion of 1745 and many members of Edinburgh's aristocracy were keen to align themselves with George III and away from Jacobite cause. The streets were therefore named after the Royal family or for aspects of the union such as patron saints (St Andrew and St George) and emblems (rose and thistle).

At first it was difficult to persuade people to build in the rural setting, so a £20-premium was offered for the first person to build a home. Mr John Young accepted the challenge and erected Rose Court (later renamed Thistle Court) off George Street. It took until 1800 to complete the first New Town and by this time, there were already calls for a second phase of development.

Register House and Waterloo Place, with a horse-drawn omnibus in the foreground, by J.G. Tunny, 1854. This is a view of the east end of Princes Street as it joins Waterloo Place. Named after Wellington's victory at the Battle of Waterloo in 1815, Waterloo Place sits atop the Regent Bridge. Its Greek-revival style was designed by Archibald Elliot and forms a perfect frame for the monuments on Calton Hill.

Statue of Wellington at Register House by Francis M. Chrystal, *c.* 1912. The dramatic statue of the Duke of Wellington is sited in front of Register House and was unveiled in 1852 on the anniversary of Wellington's victory against the French at Waterloo. To enable the enormous statue, on its red Aberdeen granite plinth, to fit, the surrounding walls and stairs of Register House had to be pushed back. It is one of the many examples of the sculptor Sir John Steell's work that grace the streets of Edinburgh. The newspapers at the time created the pun, 'the Iron Duke in bronze by Steell', as a nickname for the new sculpture.

Perspective view of the bridge and Register Office by J. Donaldson, from Hugo Arnot's *History of Edinburgh*, 1779.

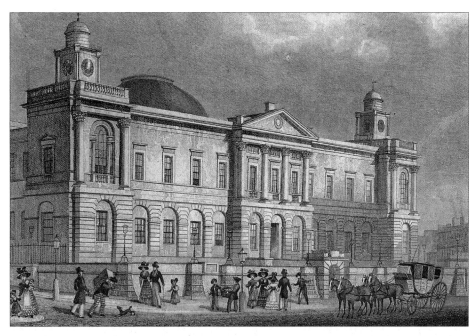

Register Office on Princes Street by T.H. Shepherd, 1829. The building of the Register Office to hold the public records of Scotland was a long, drawn-out affair. An Act in 1752 allowed for the building to be constructed but, due to lack of funds for the project, it was not until 1774 that the foundation stone was laid. It was designed by Robert and James Adam to provide a magnificent edifice to greet people as they travelled over the North Bridge. Unfortunately, funds ran out again in 1778, leaving the building with a roof on but little else. As Hugo Arnot said, it became the 'most magnificent pigeon house in Europe'. By 1788 however, it was finally made habitable and much of the Adam brothers' original plans were realised with the rear being completed in the 1820s. The building is now known as Register House.

East end of Princes Street from the front of the Theatre Royal by J.G. Tunny, 1854. The lights of the Theatre Royal can be seen on the left-hand side of this image and they are appropriately topped with miniature crowns. This photograph was taken five years before the theatre was demolished to build the General Post Office. Across the street, newspaper posters next to Crown Hotel include the announcement of 'The Battle of the Alma' fought on 20 September 1854, during the Crimean War.

Princes Street at the junction with the North Bridge, 1895. This entire block of buildings was demolished a year after this photograph was taken to make way for the building of the North British Hotel. The railings of the Waverley Market can just be seen to the right.

Left: East end of Princes Street from the Scott Monument by Thomas Begbie, 1857.

Below: Princes Street looking towards Calton Hill, *c.* 1895 – before and after images of the site of the Waverley Market which was built 1874-6. This was always the site of many markets in Edinburgh, but the building of the Waverley station had left a much smaller area for such activities and so this cast-iron structure was built to house the vegetable market. As well as gardens on the roof, there were glazed 'wells' to let light into the market beneath.

The east end of Princes Street from the Waverley Bridge by Alexander Wilson, *c.* 1890. The view from the Waverley Bridge is very different today. Gone are the imposing Edinburgh Hotel and adjoining buildings which have been replaced by a very modern sandstone and glass construction. The building housing the Old Waverley Hotel to the left, however, still remains.

The east end of Princes Street from Princes Street Gardens by Alexander Wilson, *c.* 1890. The shop in the centre with the royal crest and bay-window structure is Romanes & Paterson at 62 Princes Street. They have been trading here since 1808 and are unfortunately the only building in this image that still survives.

Left: Palace Picture House by J. Campbell Harper, 1955. Sited at 15 Princes Street, the Palace Picture House opened in 1913. This photograph was taken the year the cinema closed to be replaced by an extension to the Woolworth's store.

Below: Princes Street from the east by Postcard Photo Series, *c.* 1930. Showing the view from the North British Hotel of the Old and New Towns, this image illustrates some of the connections that were built to link the two: in the foreground, the Waverley Bridge, the Mound in the centre and, at the back, the Caledonian Hotel sitting on Lothian Road. It also gives a very clear picture of the layout of the Waverley tracks and how they go under the National Gallery of Scotland.

Princes Street from the west by G.W. Wilson, 1866. This is a very early photograph of Princes Street
life with the Edinburgh Hotel on the left-hand side. The future site of the North British Hotel and the
Waverley Market can be seen on the right. This image is also a good example of the varied forms of
horse-drawn transport that could be seen on the streets of Edinburgh and included basic carts, carriages
and omnibuses.

Left: The front of the east portion of the Old Waverley Hotel by George Morham, *c.* 1870. The ornate façade of the Old Waverley Hotel no longer exists; it was removed sometime over the next twenty years and remodelled to look like an extension of the building on the left. This building still operates today under the same name. In 1870, it was an example of one of the many temperance hotels that existed in Edinburgh. The temperance movement was one way the growing middle class attempted to influence the lower classes and mould them into an image of themselves. Many believed that alcohol was the downfall of the lower classes and they preached moderation (rather than total abstinence). They were encouraged to pursue other more middle-class pursuits, such as attending lectures, libraries and religious participation.

Opposite below: Princes Street looking west by Reliable Series, *c.* 1903. A busy Princes Street, still with its plethora of horse-drawn vehicles. Where buses stop today in front of the Waverley Market, there was once a taxi and omnibus stand.

Above: Royal Hotel, Princes Street by Alexander Inglis, *c.* 1890. The Royal Hotel once stood where Marks & Spencer and the extension to Jenners department store now are. The only recognisable building today is Romanes & Paterson.

Right: Princes Street and the corner of South St Andrew Street, *c.* 1890. This image, taken from the top of the Waverley Market, shows the future site of R. W. Forsyth's department store, which was built in 1906. At this point however, 30 Princes Street was owned by Mossman & Sons jewellers.

Left: Corner of Hanover Street and Princes Street, *c.* 1900. This image shows a haberdashery store on the corner of Hanover Street and Princes Street, with several awnings to protect the stock in the window. Above it is the studio of Edward Reuben Yerbury, the famous Edinburgh photographer, who operated here from 1864–1912.

Below: The Edinburgh Hotel from Princes Street Gardens by Alexander Wilson, *c.* 1890. The Edinburgh Hotel operated on Princes Street from 1863–1894. Prior to this, it was the Star Hotel but changed purpose completely when it became Renton's furnishing store.

Princes Street from the west at the Mound, 1903. This incredibly clear, early image shows a horse-drawn taxi standing beside the Royal Institution and the view along Princes Street. It also shows the gardens, with three of the eight monuments that inhabit its grounds. Furthest back is the Scott Monument, followed by the statue of Adam Black, the publisher and Lord Provost of Edinburgh. Behind the trees is the monument to John Wilson, the writer and professor, who died in 1854.

Princes Street from the west at the Mound, 1903. Taken on the same day as the image above, this photograph, also from the Royal Institution, shows the Princes Street shops including Romanes & Paterson and Jenners.

Masonic procession on Princes Street, 1896. The top hats and regalia of the masons can barely be seen through the crowds of people filling the street. The occasion was to mark the laying of the foundation stone for the new North Bridge on 25 May 1896.

Life Association of Scotland, Princes Street, c. 1890. This is an image of the very ornamental façade of the Life Association of Scotland's headquarters at 82 Princes Street. The company was founded in 1839 and construction on this site began in 1855. The building was designed by David Rhind and Sir Charles Barry. Rhind was also a photographer and took many photographs of Rome during a visit there. It is likely that his visit to the city influenced the strongly Roman design of this building. The Life Association building has now been demolished.

Right: The new premises of Messrs Redfern at 31/32 Princes Street by George Washington Browne, 1893. This building was designed in 1892 for Messrs J. Redfern & Son, ladies' tailors who, according to their advertisements, were 'by special appointment to the principal royal and imperial courts of Europe'. It was quite unusual to be a global tailors' company, but they were very successful, with shops in London, Paris, Nice, Cannes and New York. George Washington Browne was also the architect of the Royal Hospital for Sick Children and the Central Library.

Below: Princes Street from the west, *c.* 1858. This picture was probably taken early in the morning as the street is virtually deserted, apart from a horse-drawn cart. The large statue of Queen Victoria atop the Royal Institution was placed there in 1844, eighteen years after the building was opened.

John Ford & Co., glass and china merchants, c. 1909. John Ford & Co. were a very successful Edinburgh company. Founded in 1815, their Holyrood Flint Glass Works made cut and engraved glass that was exported all over the world.

The interior of R. & T. Gibson, Princes Street, 1935. Robert and Thomas Gibson Ltd were provisions merchants and grocers to the royal court. Their business operated from Princes Street for over 100 years from 1849-1951.

Jenners, Princes Street, 1895. Jenners is one store that has survived the passage of time. It opened in 1837 as Kennington & Jenner but was renamed Charles Jenner & Co. in 1861. A devastating fire reduced the original building to ashes in 1892, resulting in the construction of the building we see today. The new store fully opened in 1895, the year this picture was taken. Jenners remained a family-run company until 2005 when it was sold to the House of Fraser.

MacKay & Chisholm jewellers, 1905. Operating from 57 Princes Street, MacKay & Chisholm were another long-standing Edinburgh company. Established in 1826, they moved to these premises in 1878 from the North Bridge. They were quality goldsmiths who specialised in Scottish jewellery and found that the Princes Street site served them well, as there they were mostly patronised by tourists.

Above: Thornton & Co., 78 Princes Street, *c.* 1895. This company were patentees, water-proofers and India rubber manufacturers. They were founded in Edinburgh in 1848 but were so successful they ended up with branches in London, Leeds, Bradford and Belfast.

Left: The corner of Princes Street and Castle Street by Francis M. Chrystal, *c.* 1912. This view of Princes Street shows Summers and McIntyre Ltd, a stay, corset and bandage-maker, who appear to be going out of business. They had occupied this shop since the 1870s. Recently this site has been occupied by a fast-food restaurant.

View down Castle Street from George Street by Francis M. Chrystal, 1905. This image shows people walking along Princes Street. The view is unaltered today, except for the addition of a statue in Princes Street Gardens to Dr Guthrie, the philanthropist who established schools for poor and destitute children in Edinburgh.

Sir Walter Scott's house on North Castle Street by J.L.A. Evatt, 1955. The three-storey house to the right of this photo is 39 North Castle Street. It was built and occupied by Sir Walter Scott from 1801-26. He was forced to move from here when he went bankrupt due to the business failure of his publisher, John Ballantyne.

Junction of Princes Street and Castle Street, *c.* 1910. This view along Princes Street shows how the original houses would have had a basement-well in front of them, giving access to the lower part of the building. The image also shows the ornate lampposts that were once part of the street.

Right: Princes Street from the west by Joseph W. Ebsworth, *c.* 1846. This very early etching depicts the west end of Princes Street, already with a great number of shops occupying the street. These include John Menzies' first shop at 61 Princes Street where he operated as a bookshop, stationer and print-seller. It also shows that commercial ventures were not just restricted to shops within the New Town and, as with the Old Town, sellers peddled their wares on the street too.

Below: Princes Street looking east from the west end, *c.* 1915. This view along Princes Street was probably taken from the buildings on the corner of Rutland Street. The edge of St John's Episcopal church is on the right. As well as various forms of horse-drawn transport, a line of men carrying sandwich boards can be seen making their way along the street.

St John's church at the corner of Lothian Road – showing the view of Lothian Road from Maule's Corner, 1910. Lothian Road was constructed in 1785 to link the west end of the New Town to Tollcross. This photo was taken the year an architectural competition was launched to design the Usher Hall, the famous concert hall on Lothian Road.

West end of Princes Street, with the fountain in the centre, by Francis M. Chrystal, *c.* 1912. This image, taken from street level, was again taken from Rutland Street. To the left of the picture, in the middle of the road, stands a stone water fountain. This was installed by the Edinburgh philanthropist Catherine Sinclair, who gifted many drinking fountains to Edinburgh. It was removed, no doubt due to the obstruction it caused to traffic.

The Osborne Hotel, west end of Princes Street, *c.* 1877. This photograph was taken a couple of years before the Osborne Hotel was badly damaged by fire, leading to its closure. In 1904 however, it became Robert Maule & Co. department store.

Above: St Cuthbert's church, *c.* 1890. This image was taken before St Cuthbert's was rebuilt in 1893 and shows the church as it was created in the 1700s. There has been a church on this site since the twelfth century, but it was completely rebuilt in 1774, with its tower and steeple being finished in 1775 and 1789 respectively. Today only the steeple is recognisable in the architect Hippolyte J. Blanc's nineteenth-century redesign.

Left: Gardeners in St Cuthbert's churchyard by Francis M. Chrystal, *c.* 1920. Taking a rest from their toil, the gardeners of St Cuthbert's church stop for a photograph. The extended and redesigned church can be seen in the background.

St John's Episcopal church, west end by Francis M. Chrystal, *c*. 1912. St John's was built on the site of a market garden and constructed between 1816-8. The Gothic perpendicular design was created by William Burn, who is said to have derived inspiration from the English buildings of St George's chapel, Windsor and Westminster Abbey. Prior to its opening in 1818, the open crown that was atop the tower at the west end was destroyed in a storm. Perhaps this was taken as a sign, as it was never replaced.

St Andrew Square, George Street and York Place, c. 1930. This aerial view shows St Andrew Square surrounded by the grid-like streets of the New Town. In the centre of the square stands the Melville Monument, a tribute to Henry Dundas, Viscount Melville. He was an eighteenth-century politician of such standing that he was nicknamed 'Harry IX, uncrowned King of Scotland'. To the rear of the square, the St James development and Leith Street can be seen prior to the demolition of most of this area in order to create the bus station and St James shopping centre.

East side of St Andrew Square by Thomas Shepherd, 1830. Only a couple of buildings in this view are still recognisable – the two buildings with Ionic columns on either side of what looks like a gap in the street. These buildings were designed by James Craig, the architect of the New Town, and were to flank a church that was to be constructed between them. Instead of the church though, Dundas House was built, which is now occupied by the Royal Bank of Scotland, as is the building to its left. The building to the right is also owned by the bank.

The Gladstone Memorial in St Andrew Square, 1955. This memorial honours William Ewart Gladstone, who was Prime Minister four times between 1868 and 1892. Despite being born in Liverpool, Gladstone served as MP for Midlothian for much of his political career in the Liberal Party. This statue was unveiled in 1917, nineteen years after his death. It was moved to Coates Crescent Gardens in 1955, no doubt because of the increase in traffic around St Andrew Square.

Statue of Alexander and Bucephalus at the intersection of St Andrew Square and George Street, *c.* 1890. This statue was created in 1883 by Sir John Steell, like so many other Edinburgh monuments. It was moved around 1916 to make way for the Gladstone Memorial and sited in the front of the City Chambers on the Royal Mile.

Left: The British Linen Bank, St Andrew Square, floodlit by Robin A. Hill, 1966.

Below: Boys' Brigade performance in St Andrew Square, *c.* 1906. Both these images depict the British Linen Bank at 36-9 St Andrew Square. This was not in the original plan for the square, but built later in 1851-2, to a design by David Bryce. The classical building is topped off with six female statues representing navigation, commerce, manufacture, art, science and agriculture.

Right: YMCA, 14 South St Andrew Street, 1914. This is an image of the Edinburgh Young Men's Christian Association building being demolished. The YMCA had occupied this building since the 1870s, but obviously, it no longer suited their purposes. They moved temporarily to Meuse Lane just off South St Andrew Street until a new building was erected on the site of the old one.

Below: The Royal Bank of Scotland, St Andrew Square by Francis M. Chrystal, *c.* 1900. Dundas House was built for Sir Laurence Dundas, a businessman, in 1772-4. The Dundas family, however, only lived in the house for thirteen years as, following Laurence's death, it was sold to the government who used it as an excise office. In 1825, it was bought by the Royal Bank of Scotland, whose possession it remains today.

St Andrew Square Gardens and the base of the Melville Monument by Archibald Burns, *c.* 1870. The impressive-looking Melville Monument stands 150ft tall above St Andrew Square and was based on Trajan's Column in Rome. The column was built in 1821 and topped by Dundas' statue (a mere 14ft tall) in 1828.

Opposite above: Corner of South St David Street and St Andrew Square, *c.* 1910. The building on the corner is Harrison & Son, clothiers and outfitters. Their shop was at 8 St Andrew Square and 19-21 South St David Street from the late 1890s to 1910.

Opposite below: Corner of St Andrew Square and Rose Street by Dean of Guild, *c.* 1950. This building was occupied by the Scottish Widows Fund Office in the nineteenth century, following the collapse of the Western Bank who had previously owned the building. It was later demolished to be replaced by a modern construction that now houses a Sainsbury's supermarket.

Left: An atmospheric photograph of horse-drawn cabs on George Street, *c.* 1880. The street appears to be empty until you realise that it was taken with a long exposure, leaving slight, ghostly figures where people were walking along the street.

Below: Thistle Court by Joyce M. Wallace, *c.* 1987. This should probably have been the first image within this book, as Thistle Court was the first house built in Edinburgh's New Town. Originally called Rose Court, this was the site in 1767 where John Young built his mansion. It must have required quite a leap of faith by Mr Young to build in what was essentially the middle of nowhere; James Craig himself offered encouragement by laying the foundation stone.

Members of the Edinburgh University cycling club in George Street, on occasion of Scottish Cycling Meet, Saturday 14 June 1884. Is this perhaps the most amazing sight seen on George Street? A flotilla of penny farthings draws attention from the passers-by on their way towards Charlotte Square. The formation of the Edinburgh Amateur Bicycle Club in 1870, just one year after the invention of the penny farthing, shows the interest generated by this new sport within the city.

Left: The Commercial Bank of Scotland, 14 George Street by H.D. Wyllie, 1953. Built in 1847, on the site of the Old Physician's Hall, stands the Commercial Bank. The imposing classical structure was designed by David Rhind and its frontage includes six columns, 35ft tall. Through a series of mergers, the building became part of the Royal Bank of Scotland and remained so until 1993. It was then converted into a restaurant, bar and conference complex called the Dome.

Below: George Street and the statue of Pitt, 1870. This statue represents William Pitt, who was Prime Minister at the time the New Town was being constructed. Known as Pitt the Younger, he was the youngest ever Prime Minister, assuming the role at the tender age of twenty-four. It was sculpted by Sir Francis Chantrey and erected in 1833.

George Street looking west, 1908. The tall building on the right is Gray's of George Street, one of the few businesses that continue to operate from this street since this image was taken. Established in 1818, James Gray & Son Ltd moved to George Street around the time this photograph was taken and have sold hardware, home-ware and garden goods from here ever since. The building is unaltered, except for the statue which has been removed from the top.

George Street, looking east at the junction of Frederick Street, c. 1905. Frederick Street was named after the second son of King George, Frederick Augustus. William Pitt's statue looks down Frederick Street towards Princes Street.

Hanover Street by City Engineers Dept, 1958. Here, the statue of King George IV looks down Hanover Street towards the Old Town. The statue was erected in 1831 and created by Sir Francis Chantrey. The image of the King is 12ft tall and the granite plinth 18ft; required the help of cranes to set them in place.

The Assembly Rooms on George Street by Thomas H. Shepherd, 1829. The Assembly Rooms were built to provide the gentry of the New Town with an establishment for socialising. The facilities developed over time with the foundation stone being laid in 1783 and alterations to the façade in 1817 creating the Greek portico entrance. It was found necessary to extend the building and a music hall was added in 1843. The Assembly Rooms are still a major venue for Edinburgh's events today, including the Hogmanay celebrations and the Edinburgh Fringe Festival.

Right: An image capturing the demolition of 73 George Street by Edinburgh Photographic Society, *c.* 1907. The building appears to have been one of the original houses on the street that has had a shop front added on the ground level. The Gresham Life Assurance Society took down this building and erected a new one to house shops and offices that were to be rented out.

Below: Corner of Hanover Street and George Street by Edinburgh Photographic Society, *c.* 1900. The building on the corner here no longer exists; it was replaced by a much grander domed building in the early twentieth century that was constructed by the Royal Society of Edinburgh. Previously their home had been the Royal Institution on the Mound (now the Royal Scottish Academy).

West end of Thistle Street, looking east by S.G. Jackman, 1951. This photograph reveals the not-so-grand side of the New Town. Built into his grid of upper-class housing, James Craig designed a network of streets and lanes that ran between them. These provided an area for back entrances to the houses, stabling and shops to supply the New Town. The buildings here, therefore, lack the design features that characterise the main streets.

An image of 180 Rose Street by T.C.A. Inglis, 1953. From its outside demeanour, most people would not guess that this building had been frequented by royalty. However, this was near where King Edward VIII (then the Prince of Wales) used to play badminton in the 1930s and this building housed the shower baths which he used. Apparently, the boiler is still in the basement.

Rose Street, *c.* 1890. Rose Street was another of the secondary streets of the New Town. It was named in conjunction with Thistle Street, its mirror counterpart in Craig's design – they represented the floral symbols for Scotland and England. As in 1890, this street is still home to a great many bars and public houses.

Charlotte Chapel, Rose Street North Lane, *c.* 1912. Originally home to a Scottish Episcopalian congregation, the chapel became vacant when they moved to St John's on Princes Street. In 1816 however, a Baptist church took over the building. By 1907, their congregation had outgrown the chapel; it was demolished and a larger building erected in its place, opening in 1912. The Charlotte Chapel Independent Baptist Church still has its home here today.

Corner of North Charlotte Street and Queen Street by S.G. Jackman, 1951. The building on the corner remains the same today, even having the same shop frontage. Then it was St Cuthbert's store but now it is the Drum and Monkey public house.

Corner of Forres Street (left), Albyn Place (centre), North Charlotte Street (right) by S.G. Jackman, 1951. This junction represents a meeting point of two of Edinburgh's New Towns. North Charlotte Street was part of the original New Town and development began in the 1780s. However, Albyn and Forres Streets were part of the Moray Estate and the lands were not feued until 1822.

Catherine Sinclair Monument, *c.* 1900. Completed in 1868, four years after her death, this monument celebrates the life and work of Catherine Sinclair. She was the daughter of Sir John Sinclair, the Scottish politician and writer of the Statistical Account of Scotland. Catherine went on to become an author in her own right but this monument represents the respect she gained from her many philanthropic works in Edinburgh. Amongst other things, she set up cooking depots for the poor, installed drinking fountains and established a mission station in Leith.

Queen Street by H.D. Wyllie, 1953. This section of Queen Street remains virtually unchanged. The twin finials of what was originally St Luke's free church (or Queen Street church, as it was also known) can be seen towards the left of the block. Although the frontage remains, the body of the church was demolished in 1978. The building has now been turned into a gym.

Edinburgh's Ladies College, c. 1903. Queen Street was the home of Edinburgh's Ladies College from 1871-1966. This was just one of a series of moves and name changes for the institution that started life in 1694 as the Maiden Hospital in the Cowgate. In 1944, the college's name changed again to Mary Erskine's School, reflecting the name of the original creator of the Maiden Hospital.

Edinburgh's Ladies College, 70-73 Queen Street, *c.* 1910.

Edinburgh's Ladies College, 70-73 Queen Street, *c.* 1910. Mary Erksine, the founder of the Maiden Hospital was, by any standards, an extraordinary woman of her time. Following the death of her second husband, James Hair, she continued his herb business from the Old Physic Gardens before extending her interests into private banking. The fortune she made was channelled into the education of women which, in the seventeenth century, was a very forward-thinking venture.

An image of 64 Queen Street, 1959. The exterior of much of Queen Street has remained unaltered since it was constructed and can give us an impression of what Princes and George Streets must have looked like when they were first built. Here we see a typical classically-inspired New Town doorway with an intricate fanlight. This was originally the townhouse of the Earls of Wemyss.

Royal College of Physicians, 1956. Previously sited on George Street, the Royal College of Physicians moved to Queen Street in 1844. Their new premises were smaller than the grand Old Physician's Hall but again, adopted a classical architectural style, with an ornate columned portico. The portico is adorned with three appropriate statues representing Hippocrates (a Greek physician), Aesculapius and Hygeia (the god and goddess of health).

Right: Design for decoration of the porch of the National Portrait Gallery by William Birnie Rhind, 1893. The Scottish National Portrait Gallery was opened in 1889, having been funded by John Ritchie Findlay, owner of the *Scotsman*, and designed by the architect Sir Robert Rowand Anderson. This drawing from the journal *Academy Architecture* is by the sculptor William Birnie Rhind and it forms part of the highly ornate exterior decoration which includes life-sized sculptures of characters from Scotland's past. An unusual building in the Georgian street, it was constructed in red sandstone and its Gothic design was based on the Doges Palace in Venice. The Gallery collects portraits of Scots and houses the Scottish National Photographic Collection.

Below: Charlotte Square by Edinburgh Photographic Society, 1906. This view shows the west and north sides of Charlotte Square, surrounding the gardens in the centre. The square was named after Queen Charlotte Sophia, wife of George III and grandmother of Queen Victoria. Queen Charlotte was of African ancestry, being descended from the Portuguese de Sousa family. There are several paintings of Queen Charlotte by the Edinburgh artist Allan Ramsay, who was given the role of principal painter to the King in 1767.

Albert Memorial by Alexander A. Inglis, *c.* 1890. This magnificent bronze statue of Prince Albert, the consort of Queen Victoria, was erected in 1876, fifteen years after his death. The equestrian statue of the prince was sculpted by Sir John Steell and sits atop a granite plinth with sculpted side-figures by David Watson Stevenson and William Brodie. The memorial was opened by Queen Victoria herself.

Opposite above: West side of Charlotte Square and St George's parish church by Francis M. Chrystal, *c.* 1912. St George's parish church was built between 1811-4 to a design by Robert Reid. A more elaborate building by Robert Adam was forgone as it was deemed to be too costly. This church was to mirror the position of another church in St Andrew Square. Unfortunately the land was feued for a house, meaning that the church had to be built in George Street instead, somewhat spoiling the balance of the intended design.

Opposite below: North side of Charlotte Square by Francis M. Chrystal, *c.* 1912. The north side of Charlotte Square contains the property known as 'the Georgian House', which has been owned by the National Trust for Scotland since 1966 and is open to the public. The house is furnished in period style and presents a portrait of what the property would have been like when first used as a residence in 1796. The palace-front façade of the building was designed by Robert Adam and the house built for the landowner, John Lamont of Lamont.

Charlotte Street flower-seller by Dorothy Young, 1956. Charlotte Street is split into north and south, being divided by the east side of Charlotte Square. This image was submitted as part of the Edinburgh Public Libraries Photography Competition in 1956, which added greatly to the Edinburgh Room's collection of images of Edinburgh people.

An image of 6 Charlotte Square by H.D. Wyllie, 1953. This is Bute House, the official home of the Scottish First Minister. The land was first sold to a shoemaker called Orlando Hart in 1792, and in the early twentieth century was purchased by the Marquis of Bute, hence the name Bute House. The National Trust for Scotland took ownership of the property in 1966 and it then became the residence of the Secretary of State for Scotland.

four

Northern
New Town

There was no reason not to build on the success of the original New Town. Unlike the Old Town there were no physical barriers to the expansion of the new city; to the north, east and west of the New Town lay open land, estates and a scattering of small villages. From now on, much of the building development was fuelled and funded by private individuals or companies rather than solely masterminded by the town council. The council however, did have a hand in the second main phase of the New Town. In conjunction with the Heriot Trust, they planned for the development of the land to the north of Queen Street (which was mostly owned by the Heriot Trust).

This Northern New Town was planned by Sir Robert Reid and William Sibbald in 1802. It stretched from the village of Broughton to three quarters of the way down Queen Street. Some of its main arteries are continuations of James Craig's earlier streets; Howe Street of Frederick Street and Dundas Street of Hanover Street, etc. Reid and Sibbald, however, did not simply replicate the original scheme; they developed a very different style. Perhaps a sign of the confidence and pride resulting in the remodelling of their city, the Northern New Town was an altogether more flamboyant construction. The austere, grid-like design was replaced with the softer curves of Abercromby and Drummond Places and the extrovert Royal Circus. The buildings too were grander; it was a statement of the fact that Edinburgh was back on the map, once again 'the' place to live.

The development was built on steeply sloping land so the plan required ingenuity in design. William Playfair was brought in to design the marvellous Royal Circus which was on an awkward slope and St Stephen's church. Building began at Heriot Row in 1802 and the scheme was nearly completed by the late 1820s. Whereas James Craig's New Town developed into a commercial centre rather than a residential area, the Northern New Town has remained truer to its original concept. Many of the houses may have been split into flats and there are sections where businesses have moved in but generally the scheme has been left intact.

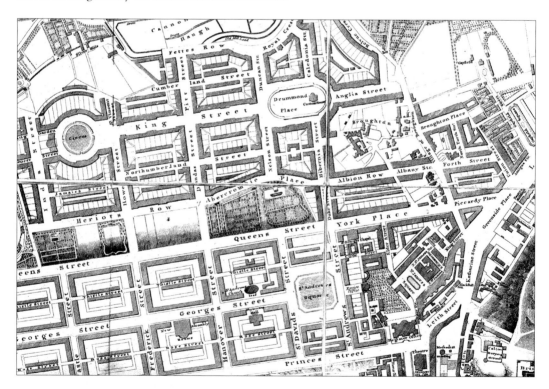

Cowan's new plan of the City of Edinburgh, 1809. This map shows the early plans for the Northern New Town. Changes were made later to the design of Royal Circus and Drummond Place. Names too were altered, with King Street becoming Great King Street and the Circus becoming Royal Circus.

An aerial view of India Street, Royal Circus, Drummond Place, Queen Street, *c.* 1930. Here, the impressive circle of Royal Circus is linked to the horseshoe-shaped Drummond Place by the broad expanse of Great King Street. To their right, Queen Street Gardens create a break between the first New Town and its northern partner.

Great King Street looking east, *c.* 1910. As George Street was to be the main street in the first New Town, Great King Street was to be its mirror in the Northern New Town. Again, named after George III, it was to be the broadest street, comprising of four palace-fronted blocks. Built in 1820, there was originally to be an impressive statue of George III astride a horse at the western end of the street, but the money required for its building was never fully raised. Great King Street is now home to the Edinburgh Photographic Society.

Bellevue House (later the Excise Office) from the *Edinburgh Magazine, c.* 1799.

Excise Office in Drummond Place by Thomas H. Shepherd, 1829. These two images show Bellevue House, as seen before and after the building of Drummond Place. The house was built in the mid-eighteenth century for General John Scott of Balcomie and Bellevue, after the General had purchased the land from Provost George Drummond in 1757. In 1802, the house was sold to the Customs and Excise Office and the land surrounding it was feued six years later, leading to the development of Drummond Place. The house was demolished in 1846 during the construction of the Scotland Street Rail Tunnel.

The view up India Street with Circus Gardens on the left and Gloucester Place on the right, *c.* 1900. The street was named after the then British colony of India.

Gloucester Place from Circus Gardens.   *Edinburgh.*

Gloucester Place from Circus Gardens by J. McCulloch & Co., *c.* 1910. The beautiful railings and lamp standard of Circus Gardens can be seen, looking out onto Gloucester Place. Gloucester Place was built between 1822-4 and, although we would consider it an expensive area today, then it was viewed as a non-fashionable street, secondary to the grand Great King Street and George Street.

Part of Royal Circus by Thomas Shepherd, 1830.

Royal Circus Hotel, c. 1950. These two views show parts of the perfectly circular Royal Circus, designed by William Henry Playfair. This street was one of the first to be built in this shape in Edinburgh, following on from the fashionable streets of Bath. The design, however, provided the perfect solution for the steeply sloping site and allowed for Circus Place to cut through the middle, giving access to Stockbridge and gardens for residents on either side.

Howe Street, Northumberland Street and North East Circus Place by J. McCulloch & Co.
of Edinburgh, *c.* 1905. View showing the sleep slope down from George Street that connects
Frederick Street with Howe Street. Howe Street was named after Richard, Earl of Howe, a naval
admiral who served during the American and French Revolutions. He was very popular with the
sailors, resulting in him gaining the rather overly-familiar nickname of 'Black Dick', due to the
dark colour of his complexion.

St Stephen's church from Howe Street by Thomas H. Shepherd, 1830. St Stephen's is a dramatic
building, standing 165ft tall at the base of the steep hill of Howe Street. Built in 1826-8 to a
Romanesque design by William Henry Playfair, it has a very unusual shape – a square on an angle
set behind a tower. The church was originally to have been built in Royal Circus but, in the end,
Playfair was given this very awkward site – hence the innovative design.

Heriot Row looking east, showing oil lamp standards, by R.A. Hill, 1967. A typical row of Georgian townhouses – this picture gives us a clear view of the elements that went into the design of many of the New Town's homes: an open basement clad in roughened stone, surrounded by ornate railings and lamp standards; the ground floor with block-effect stonework; smooth stonework on the floors above; differing window designs on each floor. Although many buildings in a street would follow this same pattern of design, sometimes they would express their individuality by having a doorway supported by Ionic pillars or such like.

Royal Crescent, 1952. Royal Crescent lies on the very edge of the Northern New Town and is another of William Henry Playfair's designs. The elegantly-shaped street was built in 1823.

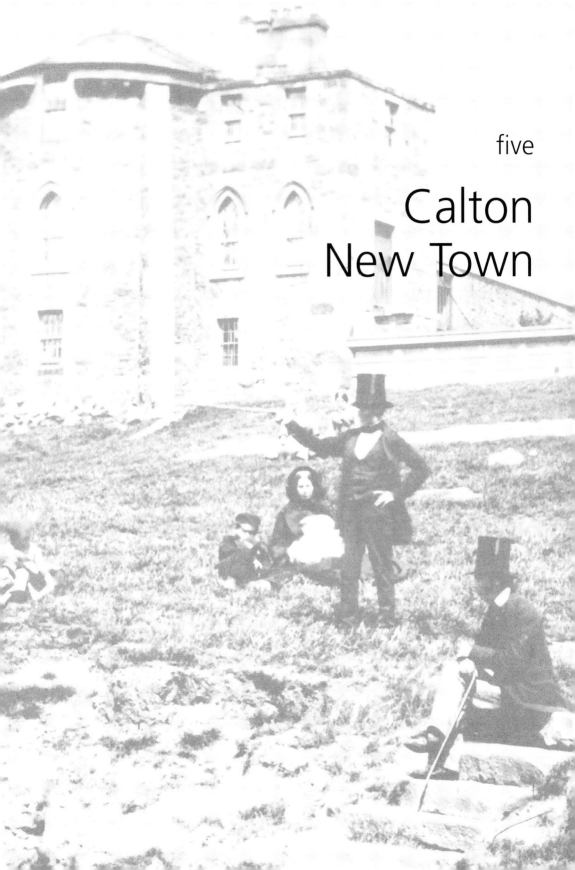

five

Calton
New Town

Calton Hill had always been a part of Edinburgh life, predominantly as a place to dry washing. It was a craggy landmark, but it is unlikely in the eighteenth century or before that it would have been conceived of as an area of national pride. Cut off from James Craig's New Town by the steep Calton ravine, it perhaps seemed equally unlikely that it would succumb to the remodelling of Edinburgh's landscape. Following Acts of Parliament in 1813 and 1814, however, it was agreed to construct a bridge to span the ravine and provide access to Princes Street from the east. Robert Stevenson (grandfather of Robert Louis Stevenson) was given the task of designing a bridge to cover the 300ft gap. This was no easy task and involved removing vast quantities of rock from the side of Calton Hill and also, driving a road through the middle of the Old Calton Burial Ground. It was named the Regent Bridge in reference to George, Prince of Wales – the Prince Regent.

With the roadway secured, a competition was held in 1815 for the design of the buildings that were to be sited on the bridge. Archibald Elliot won for his very classical design, incorporating Ionic porticos and screens, and the street became known as Waterloo Place after the British victory in 1815. The bridge and the street on top of it were open by 1817. Elliot's majestic design perhaps precipitated and intensified the developments that were to transform Calton Hill itself.

Ever since the idea of constructing an eastern approach road had been raised in 1787, the progression was to conceive of developing the land on Calton Hill and beyond. Again, a competition was held to design a development for the hill itself and all the land as far as Duke Street in Leith. However, the town council failed to choose a design, instead waiting till 1818 to grant William Henry Playfair the right to finish off a plan that he had helped William Stark begin. The scheme was dogged by setbacks and, as a result, only a portion of the thirty streets planned by Playfair were ever built. These included the aristocratic Royal, Calton and Regent Terraces, which give us an insight into how brilliant Playfair's finished scheme might have been. They cleverly follow the natural contours of the base of Calton Hill, surrounded by a veil of trees.

The rocky ground of the upper hill was unsuitable for large-scale housing development. In a perhaps unforeseen twist, it became the very focus of the New Town developments – emblematic of the national and social pride that had made the upper classes rebuild their homes and society outside the Old Town. It became a repository of monuments: monuments to great Scots like Robert Burns and Dugald Stewart; monuments to victory and bravery in wars with the Nelson and National Monuments; and testament to the Scottish scientific mind with the building of the City Observatory. Calton Hill can be viewed as a romantic folly or as another emulation of the monuments of classical Athens. It is perhaps best viewed as the city and its upper classes regaining their pride and making the most visible statement possible of their place in the world.

Waterloo Place, c. 1880. This image shows the very busy junction of Waterloo Place and the North Bridge. The grand General Post Office (GPO) building can be seen on the right. It was opened in 1866 and built on the ground previously occupied by the Theatre Royal. In Archibald Elliot's original design for Waterloo Place, the post office was to the east of the Regent Bridge and was mirrored by the stamp office to the west. This building was soon found to be too small and larger premises were sought. The GPO operated from Waterloo Place until 1995. It has now been converted into offices.

Procession of the Lord High Commissioner on Waterloo Place, 1883. Captured in this image are the crowds watching the Lord High Commissioner's procession coming down Waterloo Place, heading for the opening of the General Assembly of the Church of Scotland at Highland Tolbooth St John's church on Castlehill. The commissioner is the British sovereign's representative at the General Assembly and this is a post that still exists today. In 1883, the commissioner was John Hamilton Gordon, 1st Marquis of Aberdeen and Temair.

Waterloo Place and Calton Hill, showing Nelson Column by Francis M. Chrystal, c. 1912. Horses and carts can be seen progressing down Waterloo Place, carrying bricks and rubble. The walls of the Old Calton Burial Ground can be seen on the right; again these are designed in a Greek style with niches and Doric columns. The burial ground was opened in 1718 but plans for the building of Waterloo Place sited the new road through the middle of it. Some of the graves were therefore moved to the New Calton Burial Ground and the soil and remains were taken to their new home on carts covered with white palls.

Lower Calton showing Regent Arch by T.C.A. Inglis, 1953. Waterloo Place sits upon an amazing piece of architectural engineering – the Regent Bridge. This image, taken from Lower Calton, shows the single arch of the 50ft bridge that spans the Calton ravine. Designed by Robert Stevenson, the bridge also had to overcome the steep slope of the land and this was accomplished by building it 45ft high to the north and 64ft to the south. Open screens face either side of the bridge with Corinthian arches in the centre.

New post office, Waterloo Place by Thomas Shepherd, 1829. Previously sited on the North Bridge, Edinburgh's post office was moved to Waterloo Place in 1821. After the opening of the new GPO in 1866, this building became the Waverley Hotel.

Back of Waterloo Place and Shakespeare Square, c. 1854. This very early photograph shows the south of the Regent Bridge and the back of the buildings on Waterloo Place. The building to the far right and the street beside it are part of Shakespeare Square, which was demolished to make way for the GPO. In the foreground is part of Waverley station, this image being taken prior to the redevelopment of the station and the North Bridge which began in 1894.

Above: Calton Hill by A.A. Inglis, *c.* 1900. This image provides a bird's-eye view of Waterloo Place and Calton Hill, seen just above it. The semi-circular building at the end of Waterloo Place was the Calton Convening Rooms, which could be rented out for concerts and meetings. Today the building is a restaurant. On the right is the Old Calton Burial Ground, where the philosopher David Hume and sculptor Sir John Steell are buried. Steell was responsible for the statue of Wellington on horseback in front of Register House and the sculpture of Queen Victoria which sits on top of the Royal Institution (now the Royal Scottish Academy).

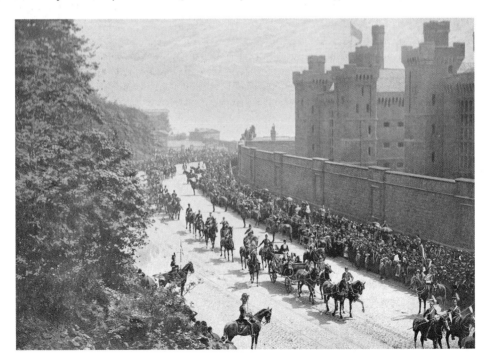

Rock House, Calton by Alexander Burns, 1874. This image shows the home and studio of photographer Alexander Burns on Calton Hill. Burns was a landscape photographer in the city from the 1850s up until the 1880s and the Edinburgh Room has many of his atmospheric photographs of Edinburgh's streets. At different times, Rock House has been home to many of Edinburgh's most famous photographers, including David Octavius Hill and Robert Adamson, the Annan brothers and members of the Inglis family.

Opposite below: 'Commissioners Walk' passing the Calton Gaol, *c.* 1880. This picture provides another view of a Lord High Commissioner's parade, this time passing the Calton Gaol on the right. The gaol was designed by Archibald Elliot, the same architect who designed the buildings on Waterloo Place. It is strange, following on from the very classical Greek-influenced street, that he designed the gaol in a castellated fashion. This may have been because he was adding to the existing Bridewell Gaol, designed by Robert Adam and completed in 1796. The Calton Gaol was in use until 1926; after this time it was demolished and replaced in the 1930s by the Art Deco St Andrew's House, home of the Scottish Office.

North British Railway from the North Bridge showing Calton Prison, 1854. Seen here from the Old Town, the rear of the Calton Gaol looks very much like a medieval castle. The two turrets in the centre are the Governor's House of the gaol and this is the only part that survived the demolition of the building prior to the building of St Andrew's House. Beneath the crags lie the houses of Lower Calton and part of Waverley station.

St Andrew's House and Nelson Monument from Canongate churchyard, c. 1940. By this time, St Andrew's House can be seen occupying the site of the Calton Gaol. Designed by Thomas S. Tait and completed in 1939, it was built as the home of the Scottish Office following their move from London. It is regarded as being a prime example of Art Deco design and is now a category A listed building.

High School by Archibald Burns, *c.* 1870. The Royal High School embodied the idea of Edinburgh as a modern Athens. Thomas Hamilton based his design for the building upon the Athenian Temple of Theseus and created the temple-like structure 400ft wide, cut deep into the face of Calton Hill. Started in 1825 and completed in 1829, the school was originally a classical seminary, specialising in ancient languages and the classics. The turreted Calton Gaol can be seen to the left of the picture.

Royal Observatory on Calton Hill by A.A. Inglis, *c.* 1890. The Royal Observatory on Calton Hill was designed by William H. Playfair and begun in 1818. It replaced a smaller observatory designed by James Craig, architect of the New Town, which was never completed due to lack of funds. Playfair's design was for a cruciform Greek temple of the winds, within its own walled compound. The observatory was visited in 1822 by George IV, who bestowed upon it the title of the Royal Observatory of King George IV. By the 1890s, however, the equipment had been left to decay and a new Royal Observatory was opened on Blackford Hill. Playfair's building was therefore renamed the City Observatory.

Washerwomen on the Calton Hill by Thomas Begbie, *c. 1858*. This picture shows a group of washerwomen and children drying laundry on the southern slopes of the Calton Hill. Many early photographs have a posed quality about them if they contain people, so it is wonderful to see this shot that has captured the ladies in a natural situation. In the background is the Old Observatory.

Opposite above: Victory Day on Regent Road and Calton Hill, 1919. Crowds gather outside the High School as the soldiers ride past. Across the road stands the Burns Monument, built in 1831 to commemorate Robert Burns, the national bard. The temple-like structure was designed by Thomas Hamilton to house a life-sized marble statue of Burns by the sculptor John Flaxman.

Opposite below: Victory Day, the view from Calton Hill, 1919. People can be seen standing on Calton Hill, watching the Victory Day parade progress down Regent Road, heading for Princes Street. It appears that canons are being fired from Edinburgh Castle and flags decorate the top of the North British Hotel (now the Balmoral Hotel).

Above: Men in top hats by the Old Observatory by Thomas Begbie, *c.* 1858. A couple of dapper gentlemen look at the view from Calton Hill. Washerwomen can be seen in the background drying clothes, as well as a group of young boys, no doubt wondering what the photographer was up to.

Opposite above: Calton Hill by Lt-Col. Batty, 1830. This early engraving depicts the well-to-do citizens of Edinburgh enjoying the surroundings of Calton Hill. Many people are out for a stroll and two gentlemen are flying kites. There is a glimpse of lower-class life with what appears to be an old soldier begging on the left-hand side. The scene is dominated by the signal-tower dedicated to Admiral Lord Nelson. After Nelson's death in 1805 at the Battle of Trafalgar, Robert Burn was asked to design a monument to his memory. His structure replaced the original 'mast' on Calton Hill and created a 106ft tall tower visible by ships in Leith. To the left of the Nelson Monument stands the National Monument or 'Edinburgh's disgrace', as it has been nicknamed. It was begun in 1822 by Charles Robert Cockrell and William Henry Playfair as a memorial to those who died in the Napoleonic Wars and was to be a copy of the Parthenon in Athens. Public funding for the project ran out and the monument was left with just twelve columns completed. On the far left of the picture, two men can be seen transporting a large block of stone up the hill towards the monument – perhaps they were hoping to finish its construction?

Below: Regent Terrace, *c.* 1960. This photograph shows a wintry Edinburgh, with just a touch of snow left on the ground. Designed by Playfair in 1825, Regent Terrace lies on the southern side of Calton Hill. The former homes are mostly holiday apartments and hotels now.

Blenheim Place, looking west by G. Kennedy, 1954. This street was named after the Battle of Blenheim in 1704, where the Duke of Marlborough gained a victory against the French. Not really an immediate connection with Edinburgh, but this gesture seems in line with the naming of Waterloo Place and the building of the Nelson Monument. The houses here are very unusual for the New Town in that they are only one storey high. The reason for this was that they were built on a precipitous slope and have been constructed above other houses that are accessed to the rear of Blenheim Place.

The west end of Royal Terrace by G.T. Kennedy, 1954. Building began in the early 1820s to the designs of William Starks and William Henry Playfair and created Royal Terrace, a street with a unique claim to fame – it is the street with the longest single façade in the city. This image shows six of the seventeen sections that make up the street's Greek-influenced design. The street is now home to many hotels.

six

Moray Estate

The Moray Estate was a thirteen-acre site with Drumsheugh House at its heart. It was surrounded by wooded parkland that sloped down to the Water of Leith in the north and was curtailed by Queensferry Road to the west. Prior to 1782, the Drumsheugh Estate was owned by the Heriot Trust, a charitable trust formed in the early seventeenth century, who bought large tracts of land in and around Edinburgh as part of an investment strategy. The estate however was sold to Francis Stuart, 9th Earl of Moray, whereupon the mansion became known as Moray House. The house passed to the Earl's son (also Francis Stuart) on his death in 1810. By this point, the estate was being bounded in the south and east by earlier New Town developments. The Earl of Moray must have realised the financial potential contained in his thirteen acres and by 1821, had decided to sell the land off for development. Rather dramatically, he began this process by demolishing the historic Moray House in 1822.

The Earl was keen to create a well-designed layout, as he himself planned to live here, and so he hired James Gillespie Graham, a well-respected architect, to work on the plans for the site. Graham was best known for his Gothic revival designs, which can be seen in his design for St Mary's Catholic chapel and his work with Augustus Welby Pugin on the Tolbooth church. A Gothic style however would not have fitted in well with the neo-classical designs displayed by the original two New Towns. Graham's classical design for the Moray Estate has met with some criticism, described by some as being repetitious and restrained. In terms of layout however, Graham created a site of immense drama. After the grid-like rigidity of the original New Town, Graham created an essay in geometry by designing a crescent (Randolph Crescent), an oval (Ainslie Place) and a twelve-sided polygon (Moray Place). They created elegant shapes upon which the aristocratic townhouses could be built. It was a very clever design, taking into consideration the steep slope of the land and also connecting with the ends of the original New Towns, forming a cohesive design.

The houses were built between 1822-55 following very strict rules about the height and layout of all constructions. It was to be an aristocratic enclave, providing homes only for the wealthy, with no commercial properties allowed to bring the tone of the area down. All the streets went on to be named after members of the Earl's family or after their estates elsewhere. The Earl of Moray built himself a new home, in the centrepiece of Graham's design, at 28 Moray Place. Today little has changed; even many of the cobbles and original paving stones remain, giving us an excellent insight into Graham's original design.

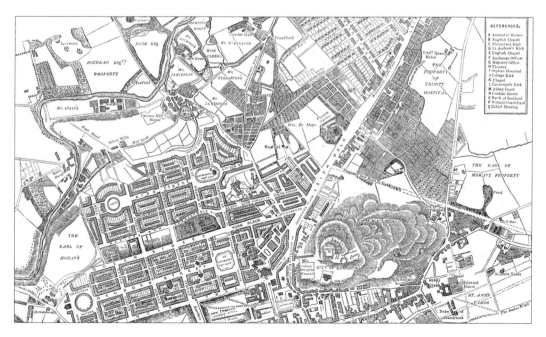

Above: Ainslie Place by Thomas H. Shepherd, 1830. This engraving is from a collection of 100 images of Edinburgh called *Modern Athens*. They were created between 1829-30 from the drawings and paintings of Thomas H. Shepherd. As well as images of Edinburgh's classically inspired New Town, it also included engravings of the Old Town and outlying buildings.

Below: Ainslie Place, south-east block looking south-west by G.J. Kennedy, 1951. Ainslie Place was named after Margaret Jane Ainslie, wife of the 10th Earl of Moray. It was built between 1826 and 1860 and constructed in an unusual oval shape around a pleasure park in the centre for residents.

Opposite: Map of the New Town by John Ainslie, 1804. This map shows the Earl of Moray's estate on the left-hand side. It clearly illustrates how the development of the estate would neatly link the first two New Towns.

The New Town, an aerial view, *c.* 1930. The circular shape of Moray Place can be seen in the left-hand corner joining the first New Town to the south at Queen Street and the Northern New Town to the right at Heriot Row.

Left: The staircase of 19 Moray Place by John Porteous, 1967. This picture provides a fantastic view up the three or four floors of 19 Moray Place. This was the home of the painter and photographer David Octavius Hill from 1837-42. He formed a famous partnership with Robert Adamson from 1843-47 and between them they created a historically important body of work documenting the people and buildings of Victorian Scotland.

Below: Moray Place by Brian Sunners, 1956. Moray Place was obviously named for the Earl of Moray's estate – the land upon which it was built.

Randolph Crescent, view from West Register House, Charlotte Square by the *Evening News*, 1975. Randolph Crescent creates a wine-glass shape, being bounded at the south-west by Queensferry Street and with the stem of Great Stuart Street leading away to the north-east. The area within the crescent that is now inhabited by gardens was previously where Drumsheugh House stood, the home of the Earl of Moray. It is believed that he originally intended to build himself a new home within the gardens but instead elected to live in Moray Place.

Albyn Place looking east by J. Campbell Harper, 1956. The stunning palace-fronted terrace design of Albyn Place was built in the early 1820s. The unusual name comes from the Gaelic word, *Albainn*, which means 'Scotland' or 'men of Scotland'.

Randolph Place by Dorothy Young, 1956. This is a view down Randolph Place to the back of St George's church. The church is now used as West Register House, part of the National Archives of Scotland. Here they store court and government records, maps and plans.

The Oratory of St Anne, Randolph Place by Louis Costello, 1957. Not quite in keeping with the classical feel of the New Town, this pretty mock-Tudor building sits in Randolph Place. Created in around 1900 by Sir Thomas Duncan Rhind, it was built as a shop. Today it is used as a restaurant and as a Polish and Italian Catholic church.

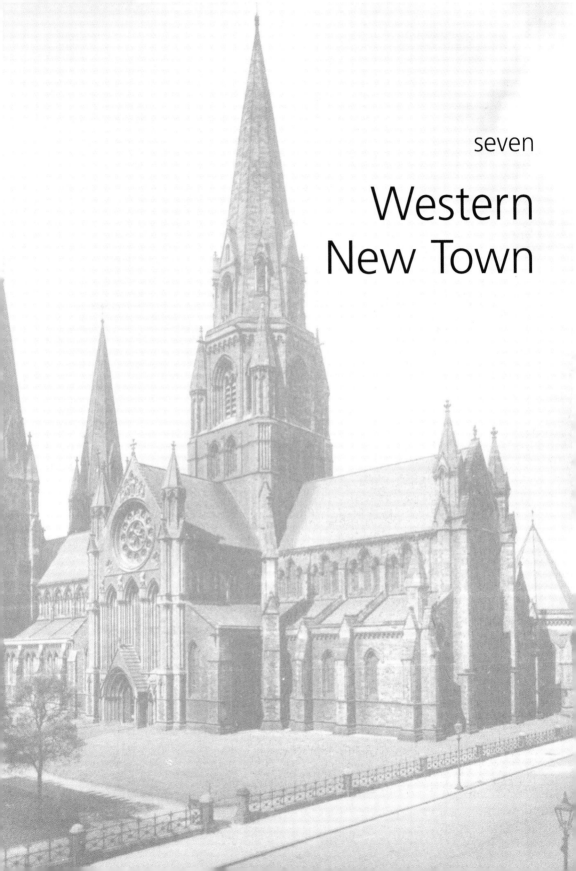

seven

Western
New Town

The Western New Town joined on to the first New Town and was a natural progression of James Craig's main artery west – Princes Street. Unlike the unified scheme for the original New Town, this was not conceived of as a singular scheme nor developed by the town council. It was constructed by a series of individuals undertaking private development. The first step was the construction of Maitland Street in 1805 by Sir Alexander Charles Maitland to connect Princes Street to the Glasgow Road at Haymarket. In 1806, a terrace of houses was built at its eastern end called Shandwick Place, and eventually this became the name for this part of the street also. Shandwick Place was flanked by the stately Coates and Atholl Crescents and this development was completed by 1825.

The land to the north of Shandwick place was part of the Coates Estate and in 1813, William Walker of Easter Coates asked the architect Robert Brown to draw up plans for the development of his lands. Brown came up with a grid plan in a similar style to the original New Town, but with an offset square at its centre. The main road for this development was the broad Melville Street, which was crossed by Walker Street (named after the Misses Walker of Coates and Drumsheugh). Mary and Barbara Walker left their fortune to the Scottish Episcopal Church for the construction of the cathedral which sits at the west end of Melville Street. In 1826, an extension was designed by James Gillespie Graham to link his plan for the Moray Estate to Brown's Coates development. This was achieved by the building of Drumsheugh Gardens, Rothesay Place and Chester Street.

Although long past the Georgian era, the development of the Wester Coates Estate from 1865 was still the continuation of a process begun in 1767. There is a complete break in design from the grid-like design of the earlier part of the Western New Town. Here the main streets of Grosvenor, Lansdowne, Eglinton and Glencairn Crescents form two large oval-shaped patterns connected at their eastern end to Palmerston Place.

West end by Alexander A. Inglis, *c.* 1890. This picture shows a bustling west end with a beautiful view of St Cuthbert's and St John's churches and Edinburgh Castle. To the right, on the corner of Shandwick Place, is a very exotic oriental bazaar displaying its wares outside. The building on the left was converted into Maule's department store shortly after this photo was taken and the corner itself became known as Maule's Corner.

Opposite: Princes Street station and the Caledonian Hotel, c. 1910. This photograph provides a great view of the original setup of the Caledonian Hotel, when it was the Caledonian Railway Station and Hotel. The Caledonian Railway was a major Scottish rail company and commenced building the station in 1894. It was built in red sandstone in a Dutch Baroque style, so was quite different from the surrounding buildings. It was a dual-purpose building with two entrances: the one on the left led to the hotel and the one on the right to the station. So close were the two functions that, at one point, steam from the trains was used to heat the hotel's water. The railway station closed in 1965, as it was no longer able to compete with trams and cars. The hotel has continued however and has developed into a five-star establishment.

Left: A beggar being passed by a woman in a hurry in Shandwick Place by Francis M. Chrystal, *c.* 1927. This photograph is quite unusual as Francis M. Chrystal was very interested in the historical buildings of the Old Town and in fact was a founder member of the Old Edinburgh Club. Many of his photographs record the buildings of the Old Town prior to their destruction. We therefore have few pictures by him that are of people. Here, he captures the moment when a well-dressed lady ignores the pleas of a city beggar for help.

Below: Shandwick Place looking west by S.G. Jackman, 1946. Taken just after the Second World War, this scene shows a busy Shandwick Place, the main road from the west connecting with Princes Street. It was named after the village of Shandwick on Easter Ross, where the owner and developer of the site came from.

West End Cinema, Shandwick Place (Albert Hall) by Kevin and Henry Wheelan, 1971. This image shows the beautifully carved door-surround of the Albert Institute of the Fine Arts. It opened in 1876 and was named after Prince Albert, the consort of Queen Victoria. The aim of the institute was to promote art in general and, in particular, contemporary Scottish art. By the 1890s, it was being used as a meeting hall and renamed the Albert Hall. In 1908 it became a cinema and shortly after, changed its name again to the West End Cinema. It operated as a cinema until 1932.

West End, the United Service Club, corner of Shandwick Place and Queensferry Street by Francis M. Chrystal, c. 1912. The Caledonian United Services Club was founded in 1825 and occupied premises in St Andrew's Square. In 1902, they moved to Shandwick Place where they continued to add to their fine library of military and naval books. It amalgamated with the Northern Club in 1954 and again, joined with the Scottish Conservative Club in 1970, leading to the sale of their premises. The new organisation was called the Caledonian Club and was based on Princes Street.

Left: St Mary's Cathedral from the north-west, *c.* 1900. Barbara and Mary Walker donated their Drumsheugh Estates to the building of St Mary's. An architectural competition was held to select a design and an entry by Alexander Ross seemed to have the popular vote. When Sir George Gilbert Scott controversially won however, he was asked to amend his design and create three spires instead of one, just like Ross's design.

Below: Melville Street by H.D. Wyllie, 1953. The picture provides a view of Viscount Melville's statue in Melville Crescent. Robert Dundas, the second Viscount Melville, was a politician who went on to be First Sea Lord of the Admiralty. His name is known around the world with both the Melville Islands in Canada and Australia being named after him. The statue is made of bronze and was created by Sir John Steell in 1857.

Right: A view of 41 Drumsheugh Gardens by H. Graham Glen, *c.* 1905. The street was named after the house of the Walker sisters (who owned the Easter Coates Estate) – Old Drumsheugh House, which was demolished in 1872, two years before the street was built.

Below: A view of 23 Melville Street (north side) by C.H. Jones, 1951. Melville Street was designed by architects Robert Brown and Gillespie Graham and constructed from 1820-30. The eastern end of the street beautifully frames St Mary's Episcopal Cathedral, which lies symmetrically between either side of Melville Street.

The drawing room of 23 Rutland Street, *c.* 1880. Dr Brown was a famous and well-liked character in Edinburgh society, known as 'the beloved physician'. As well as being a medical doctor, he was a writer and was best known for the short story about a dog called 'Rab and his Friends'. Rutland Street was the residence of Dr John Brown from 1850 until his death in 1882 and was a focal point for social and intellectual gatherings in the city.

Rutland Street by H.D. Wyllie, 1953. This image shows the northern side of Rutland Street, looking towards Princes Street. It was constructed in 1830 but the southern part of it was removed in 1869 for the formation of the Caledonian railway station.

St George's West church, Shandwick Place by Francis M. Chrystal, 1907. This photograph provides a view along Shandwick Place, towards the west end of Princes Street. The spire of St George's West church can be seen on the left. The congregation moved here in 1869 after being forced to sell their previous church to the Caledonian Railway, who needed more space for their station at the foot of Lothian Road. The new church was designed by David Bryce, the architect responsible for Fettes College and the Royal Infirmary at Lauriston Place.

Atholl Place, west end, looking towards Atholl Crescent by Kennedy, 1952. Built in the 1820s, it was probably named after John Murray, 4th Duke of Atholl, who was a prominent politician at the time.

Left: Coates Crescent, 1953. The spire of St George's West church can be seen from the arc of Coates Crescent. The street's name comes from the Coates Estate that existed prior to the building of this as well as Melville, Stafford and Walker Streets.

Below: Queensferry Street by Alexander A. Inglis, *c.* 1900. This image shows the end of Queensferry Street with the Dean Bridge at the end. Drumsheugh Gardens can be seen on the left, where the girls are carrying washing over the road. Queensferry Street was built from 1815 and constructed over the cottages of Kirkbraehead, as the road was previously called.

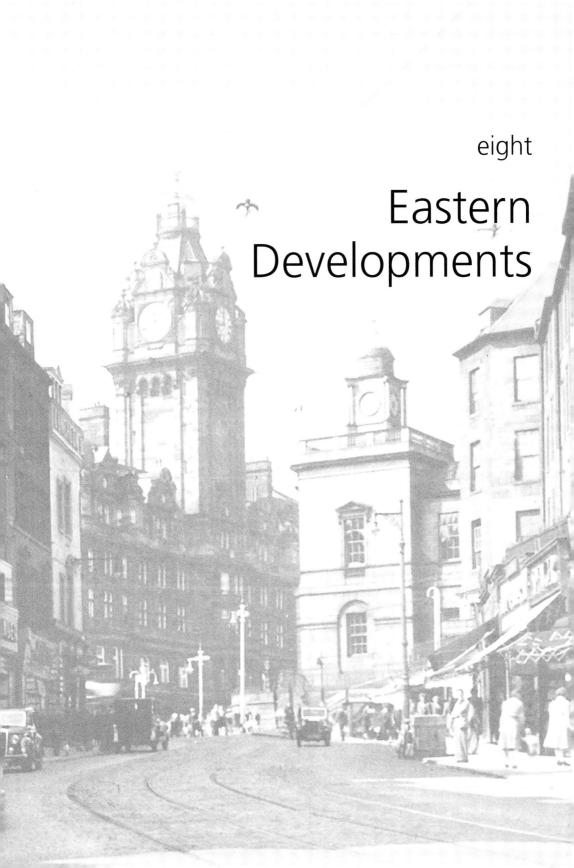

eight

Eastern
Developments

As in the west, it was natural that expansion should continue in the east. There were two obvious points that this should occur: a connection was needed for the North Bridge to be linked to the Wester Road to Leith (the road which later became Leith Walk); it also seemed logical to continue the end of Queen Street, again linking up with the Wester Road. The first of the two expansions became Leith Street and this was in fact named on James Craig's 1767 plan. Due to the geography of the land and the positioning of the existing routes, Leith Street meanders in a curve round the base of Calton Hill and on a map, looks like it was not a planned aspect of the New Town at all. Built in 1774, originally the name covered the roadway alone and the terraces upon it were named High Terrace, Catherine, Calton and Greenside Streets. Robert Adam, who designed Register House at the head of Leith Street, was asked in 1785 to design buildings for the western side of the road. Unfortunately, his elaborate designs for a raised terrace were never undertaken as it was felt that the area would not attract people of the 'right' social standing for such expensive buildings.

The land to the west of Leith Street was elevated ground, consisting of Moultray's Hill and Cleland's Yards. The owners of the yard asked James Craig to plan a redevelopment of the area and in 1775 building began on what was to become St James' Square. By 1804, the area was covered by St James' Square, Place and Street, but by the mid-1850s, it was beginning to decline, assuming the air of the Old Town rather than the New. In 1965, the St James development was almost completely cleared for the building of shops, offices and government buildings. Now, only a small section of St James' Square remains.

York Place was feued in the 1790s and shut the gap between Leith Walk and Queen Street, enclosing the St James development. Its creation allowed for a new stage of building that overran two of the oldest villages in the environs of Edinburgh: Broughton and Picardy. The early 1800s saw the removal of the ancient settlement of Broughton, which had existed since at least the twelfth century, and the construction of Albany, Barony and Broughton Streets. At the same time, the houses of Picardy, built in 1730 for a settlement of French weavers, were swept away creating Picardy Place, Forth Street, Union Place and Street.

Clelland's Gardens, St James' Place by Alexander A. Inglis, *c.* 1900. Clelland's Gardens predated the building of St James' Place and can be seen on James Craig's 1767 map of the New Town. It was known as the oldest house in the New Town and was demolished in 1904.

St James' Square by the *Edinburgh Evening News*, 1960. St James' Square was built on the top of Multrees Hill between 1775 and 1790. It was designed by James Craig, the architect of the original New Town, although in this scheme he designed the buildings themselves as well as the layout. The square's name has Jacobite references and relates to James Edward Stewart, son of the deposed King James II (James VII of Scotland), who laid claim to the English and Scottish thrones. The square was demolished in 1965 to make way for the St James Shopping Centre development.

St Paul's Episcopal church, *c.* 1880. Built with funds raised by the Cowgate Episcopal Chapel congregation, construction began in 1816 to Archibald Elliot's designs. It is one of the finest Gothic-designed churches in Scotland. It is now known as St Paul's and St George's church and is currently undergoing renovation to increase capacity for its growing congregation.

Left: Leith Street by the *Evening News,* 1952.

Below: Leith Street, *c.* 1937. The building of Leith Street became inevitable with plans for the North Bridge. For political reasons, the building of the North Bridge was promoted by the council as a better way to reach the Port of Leith rather than as a way of opening up new land in the north for building. Leith Street was therefore essential to connect the North Bridge with the Wester Road to Leith (Leith Walk). Its outline was proposed on Craig's New Town plan and building commenced in 1774. The buildings on the west side were demolished for the building of the St James Shopping Centre.

Catholic chapel seen from Picardy Place by T.H. Shepherd, 1829. The building was designed by James Gillespie Graham in 1813 and was the first new Roman Catholic chapel to be consecrated in Edinburgh since the Reformation. St Mary's status was raised to that of a cathedral in 1878 and it is now known as St Mary's Metropolitan Cathedral.

St George's chapel, York Place by Thomas H. Shepherd, 1829. This chapel was built in a very unusual Gothic octagonal design conceived by James Adam in 1794. Although this building exists today, it is practically unrecognisable; the frontage now being flat rather than octagonal and the beautiful Gothic windows replaced. The chapel is now used as a casino.

Left: Albany Street on the Coronation holiday by Edinburgh Photographic Society, 1911. The Gothic-style church was St Mary's free church which had been built on the site of a quarry. Building began in 1859 and the design, by architect J. T. Rochead, took three years to complete. The church has now been demolished.

Below: Albany Street, 1850. Albany Street continued the trend of naming streets after the royal family, being named for Frederick, Duke of York and Albany, who was the second son of George III.

Right: Interior of John Knox Robb's house, 16 Barony Street, *c.* 1920.

Below: Barony Street, *c.* 1900. Barony Street lies off Broughton Street and, in fact, takes its name from the Barony of Broughton. The building of this and the surrounding streets also saw the end of what remained of the ancient settlement of Broughton Village.

Other local titles published by Tempus

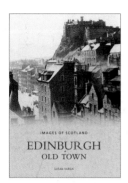

Edinburgh Old Town
SUSAN VARGA

This fascinating collection of 200 images from the Edinburgh Room represents a pictorial history of Edinburgh's Old Town. Included are all the most beautiful locations of the Royal Mile, with archive images of Castlehill, the Lawnmarket, Grassmarket, George IV Bridge and the royal residences of Holyrood House and Edinburgh Castle. Offering a unique perspective on the changing social conditions of the Old Town, the collection is a must for anyone who has been seduced by the beauty of this unique city.

978 07524 4083 5

Haunted Edinburgh
ALAN MURDIE

Explore the darkest secrets of Edinburgh's past with this collection of stories, telling of the inexplicable occurrences and ghostly apparitions that have haunted residents of the city over the centuries. Compiled by the former chairman of the Ghost Club and illustrated with more than seventy haunting images from his own collection, this book is sure to capture the imagination of any reader with an interest in the paranormal history of Scotland's capital.

978 07524 4356 0

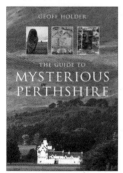

The Guide to Mysterious Perthshire
GEOFF HOLDER

A comprehensive guide to everything folkloric, supernatural, paranormal, eccentric and odd that has been recorded about the area, Mysterious Perthshire provides a fascinating introduction to the tombstones, simulacra, standing stones, gargoyles and archaeological curiosities of Perthshire. Included are tales of ghosts, fairies, witchcraft, freak weather, strange deaths and hoaxes, making it the ideal guide for armchair adventurers and on-location visitors alike.

978 07524 4140 5

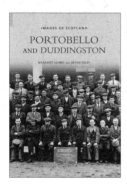

Portobello and Duddingston
MARGARET MUNRO AND ARCHIE FOLEY

This fascinating collection of over 200 images provides a pictorial history of Portobello, famous as a seaside holiday resort, and the adjoining parish of Duddingston, which still maintains its rural village life centred around the church and the loch, despite the advance of suburbia. The result is a volume which will delight anyone who has lived in, worked in or even visited Portobello or Duddingston.

978 07524 3657 9

If you are interested in purchasing other books published by Tempus, or in case you have difficulty finding any Tempus books in your local bookshop, you can also place orders directly through our website

www.tempus-publishing.com